COOMOOROO— OUR LEGACY

Never Let the Truth Get in the Way of a Good Story

Sue Kapperer

BALBOA.
PRESS

A DIVISION OF HAY HOUSE

Balboa Press books may be ordered through booksellers or by contacting:

Balboa Press
A Division of Hay House
1663 Liberty Drive
Bloomington, IN 47403
www.balboapress.com.au
1 (877) 407-4847

ISBN: 978-1-4525-1262-4 (sc)
ISBN: 978-1-4525-1263-1 (e)

Printed in the United States of America.

Balboa Press rev. date: 04/02/2014

CONTENTS

PREFACE

This is the story of my parents, Jeff and Pat Sheather, from Dad's childhood to when he met Mum and then through their lives together, until now.

It is a collection of memories from people who, I believe, have had an impact on Dad's and Mum's lives. I have attempted to build a story around these memories, but please keep in mind as you read this book that it is a collection of memories and not an attempt at revealing truths.

Memories differ from one person to another, so bear that in mind. Memories are stories told by individuals, and we all tell our own versions.

Dad has always said, "Never let the truth get in the way of a good story," and I implore you to remember that line as you read this book.

DEDICATION

To Dad and Mum,

thank you for being the parents that your are,

for the gifts you have shared,

the strength that you have shown

and the love that you continually give.

Sue xo

ACKNOWLEDGEMENTS

I want to take this opportunity to thank my husband, Eric, for his endless patience while I have been interviewing, transcribing, and writing over the past seven years. Thanks to my children, Adam and Hayley, for being my sounding boards, and to my sister Mandy and good friend Sheridan, for helping me with the editing and story lines. Thanks to all the people who have given their time and memories of Dad and Mum, which have allowed me to create this story. Thanks to my sister Carolyn, for the drawing she did from listening to one of Dad's recordings. And finally, thanks to Dad and Mum for putting up with me constantly visiting with recorder in hand, pleading for just one more memory.

CHAPTER 1
THE EARLY YEARS

Jeffery Clifford Sheather was born on 26 January 1933. He was the youngest of seven children and was always going to be a very special Australian.

His parents, Cecil Clifford (known throughtout this book as Pop) and Margaret Rita (Eliza) Sheather (née Sloan), owned a beef cattle property known as Trentside, located approximately four miles from Wodonga, Victoria, where Dad was bought up with his older siblings. Dad's eldest sibling was his sister Sylvia, followed by three more sisters, Unita, Lillian, and Betty. Then there were his brother Murray and another sister, Joceyln.

1934: Dad as a toddler

1938: Dad at front with
Lillian and Murray

Dad's mother died not long after he turned five, and so childhood was tough. He recalls his early life to us as having the occasional happy time mixed in with a lot of unhappiness and loneliness. His elder siblings disagree with this outlook, stating that they had a very happy childhood. My feeling is that given that they were quite a bit older than Dad, they may have had quite different childhood experiences. After a series of housekeepers caring for the children, Pop eventually remarried and had another child (Dale) with his second wife, Valerie Delacorn.

Aunty Joy recalls:

> My only memory of Mum is Jeff and I brushing her hair in the front bedroom of Trentside, our old family home. It was the night before she went into hospital and died—we were only told that she had gone away. I remember the day of the funeral: two aunties minded us kids, and we played under a gum tree in the horse paddock next to the cow shed.
>
> In the early years we were looked after by housekeepers who were very strict. We had to sit at the table and eat everything on our plate at meal times—yuck, cold veggies! We bathed every Saturday night, one after another, in water that was heated in the copper. On Sunday we wore clean clothes and had a good roast for lunch. Sometimes cousins would come from Albury, and we would play cricket in the front lane or swim. In later years we had boyfriends, so we created our own fun. We girls would bake on Saturdays, so we had lovely suppers on Sunday nights and played cards.

1914 - Maraget Rita Sloan
Dads mother seated 3rd from right

Betty, Joyce Dad & Murray

L-R Back - Phoebe Silva, Daphne Ingram, June Leitch, Dorothy Silva, Betty Sheather
Front - Jeff Sheather, Joy Sheather, Noelene Kinge, June Silva, Marg Silva, Laurel Janck, Laurie Melgaard
Sitting - Bill Know, Leon Wolf, Murray Sheather - Wodonga West State School 1940

Wodonga West State School - 1940

Pop 2nd from left,
Great grand dad 3rd from left

1945 - Back Row Chick Logies sister, Lillian, Unita
Middle - Betty, Dad Joyce, Val Boyes, Murray
Front - Sylvia and Jeff Quinlivan

1945 - Dad in front Aunty Nita on right

1948   1948

1945 - Dad's five sisters

MORNING MAIL, THURSDAY, OCTOBER 18, 1945

THREE WINNING TEAMS AT THE KIEWA SCHOOL SPORTS

OFF TO A FLYING START IN THE RELAY AT KIEWA

1945 - Top picture - Dad 3rd from right

1945 - Murray, Reg Pheifley and Dad

A distant relative (always referred to by Dad as Nesbit) had requested that Pop buy a horse for the youngest Nesbit son and then have Dad teach the boy to ride. When Pop purchased the horse, he told Dad to take his own horse, Corey, and lead the new horse to the Nesbit property, where he was then to live until the son was a competent rider.

The trip to Hell Hole Creek near Kergunyah took approximately sixteen hours. It was long, frustrating, and by the end quite daunting. At one stage Dad thought he had reached his destination, only to be told by the owner of the house had he stopped at that he had another six miles to go. The kindly gentleman rang Nesbit, who said he would come to escort Dad the rest of the way once he had finished his dinner. Dad was alone, hungry, and exhausted, and from the stories he has told, I believe he may have been just a little intimidated by the dark as well!

Dad recalls:

> *Nesbit got the old man to buy his son a horse, and I was to go out, take the horse out there, and teach the useless bloody son to ride. I was probably halfway between somewhere and nowhere around about midday. The pony I was leading got pig-headed and started to drag behind, and the horse I was riding was doing all the work, dragging this bugger of a pony 'cause it didn't want to walk any farther. I had a stockwhip, so I had to reach over the pony's back and lay into it with the whip handle. As time went by lumps came up, the size of the knob of the whip, over the pony's back. I was feeling somewhat guilty at this stage, as well as exhausted.*

Dad has told quite a few stories about his years at Nesbit's, and there is not one happy memory among them. He recalls there being two children, the younger one being two years younger than himself, and Dad has described him as having no gumption and being pretty dumb. Dad would start his day with a lantern in hand, go out to find and saddle his horse, get the cows in prior to daylight, and then help with the milking. He did all this before he had his breakfast, and then he rode an hour to get to school. The evenings were much the same, with cows being brought in to milk by Dad on his way home from school. As if all that wasn't tiring enough for a young boy, he also had to do an additional two-hour horse ride three evenings a week to collect the newspapers and bread from a neighbour. This really messed with his head, knowing that he had to do so much when the Nesbit children did so little.

Dad recalls:

> *I was lucky in a way, because my teacher, Mrs. Marg Kelly, boarded at Nesbit's for the first three months I lived there. She knew what sort of people they were, and although she had a "No sleeping at school" rule, she would send me out of class each day so I could have a sleep, and then she would get me back in half an hour before the end of class so the other kids didn't know about it. I don't think I would have survived without her. This was the routine of my life before I decided that enough was enough and moved on.*

Not all Dad's recollections are so favourable. He told another story about when he was twelve, and his horse Corey became really sick, with death being a serious possibility. She needed medical attention, and as she was a large horse Dad had a lot of problems trying to treat her condition. When he asked Mr. Nesbit to help, his reply was, "Why? It's not my horse." Nesbit left Dad to handle things on his own. He doesn't remember which one of them wore out first, but he ended up getting the medicine into her and then sat up with her until two or three in the morning before he knew she was going to be okay. Apparently she ended up living until she was thirty-three years old, which is a great innings for a horse. I don't recall Dad ever telling any stories of good times had while he lived with the Nesbits, and by the time he was fourteen he decided he'd had enough.

Dad recalls:

> *When school finished three years later, at the age of fourteen I packed up my gear, hopped on the horse, and rode into Wodonga with nowhere in particular to go and nowhere to stay. I suppose Cookie [Bill Cook, who had been dating my sister Nita for sometime and then later married her] just said, "Come and throw your gear at our place." That was the start of a fast friendship. I might have been bad enough at laughing, but Cookie was a shocker. Mum [this reference is to my maternal grandmother] used to call him the man with the laughing teeth. He giggled all the time.*

Dad spent just under twelve months in Wodonga working with the brothers Cookie and John, and their friend John Barker. Cookie and John's parents leased a house and land on the Hume Highway in Wodonga, where they lived and worked. At this stage of his life, Cookie was a professional horse breaker who had no trouble finding enough work for Dad. At one stage they were working up to twenty-four horses at the same time.

Cookie was one of those people who was always laughing or making those around him laugh, and if he and Dad were together, there was always trouble brewing. They were always playing practical jokes on those around them. I don't recall a time when Cookie and Aunty Nita visited us as kids that those two weren't giggling and causing mayhem.

Here are a few of Dad's memories of the times the boys spent together in their youth.

Poor old John [Barker] was always in strife. Once, with John driving, we were going down the main street [of Wodonga] heading for the Melba Theatre in a brake, when the horse's legs slid out from underneath him, and he slides across the road, and 'cause he had a fair bit of speed up, he slides straight towards the Melba Theatre. No one was seriously hurt, but boy, did we laugh!

Another time we were down the river swimming horses at Trentside. John was riding a young two-year-old on its first time out, and I was riding a grey mare that was mad. The grey mare had just been sent to us 'cause she was stuffed, and by that once a horse bolts, you can never stop them or break the habit. We went through the gate to get into the farm, and John's horse wouldn't stand, so he left me to shut the gate. This grey mare decided she'd bolt, and I went past John like that! [He slides his hands past each other]. And John's frightened two-year-old goes into the barbed wire! A trip to the hospital and seventeen stitches later, we headed back home.

Then another time with a yearling Clydesdale, John was trying to push him back into the shafts, trying to get this horse into the brake, and the horse decided to latch on to one of his boobs. It's funny, John was always

7

in the wars. John Barker was a good-looking fellow, and his mother was very strict on him. He had to brush his hair two hundred strokes a day, and his teeth one hundred strokes a day. If he would find a hair in his brush, he would go out and buy some hair restorer. Anyway, this horse decided he wasn't going to play the game, and head-butted John. Blood was running everywhere, a few teeth were broken, and all he could say was, "What will my mother say?" Cookie was killing himself laughing!

CHAPTER 2

THE MAKING OF THE MAN

While Dad was working with the boys in Wodonga, Cookie was asked to break two horses for the Docker brothers at Bontharambo, north of Wangaratta. The first year was a trial run for Cookie, but the Dockers must have been happy with his work because they offered him the job of being a regular horse breaker as required each season. The following year Dad and John Barker went down for the season to break horses, and it was during this time that Dad was offered a permanent position as a jackaroo at Bontharambo, where he then lived for approximately three years. Mr. Hubert Docker and Mr. Geoff Docker owned the Bontharambo property, which was a very well-established stud known for breeding prime thoroughbreds and Angus cattle.

Dad recalls:

> *Cookie was a horse breaker, and it was pretty hard to find a good horse breaker back then, but that was his profession. There was a song on the radio at the time that the locals adapted to honour some of the renowned rodeo riders in the area; it included a line about Cookie that went, "Billy Cook the flank rope king." But at any rate, Bontharambo had sent two horses for Cookie to try out, and they must have been pleased with him because they got Cookie and John Barker to go down and break the yearlings. They used to have about ten or fifteen to break in every year. The first year Cookie went down, and the second year Cookie sent John and me down to do them. I was there for about three weeks helping to break in the yearlings, and they offered me a job, so I took it.*

Up until then I had only been on very casual wages working for a stock agent here in Wodonga, where I did work at the saleyards and a bit of droving work for them. I got sent out to Allan's Flats one morning at 3:00 AM to get some bullocks. While driving along the road to Wodonga, I remembered that my boss said there was a couple of old bachelor fellows that used to have the cattle out there, and they said, "Tell him [Dad] to be out there at three, and we'll give him breakfast." When I get there, this fifteen-year-old kid put on black tea, bread and butter, and cold meat at three o'clock in the morning! The only reason I remembered this trip was because of the breakfast.

It was early in 1948 when Dad moved down to Bontharambo, and this was where he found his real passion for Angus cattle and their breeding. He continued to work with the horses but was also taught the finer points of beef cattle. It has been said that Dad was a horse whisperer, but that was nothing compared to what he could do with cattle.

Bontharambo was where Dad truly grew up. It was there that he learnt to cook, to take care of himself, and to become the man who would achieve so much. The work was hard but also rewarding, and it was a time to be mentored and appreciated for the skills and initiative he possessed. This was a time for Dad to grow in ways he was never given the opportunity to when living with the Nesbits or when mucking around with Cookie and the boys.

Mr. Geoff Docker had a love for thoroughbreds, and Mr. Hubert Docker loved both thoroughbreds and Angus cattle, but for both of them, what they *really* loved were the jumping races. They were both more than happy to share their knowledge with Dad, who soon soaked it all up. As well as continuing to improve his horse breaking skills, Dad's time at Bontharambo was an ongoing learning period, where he acquired many new skills. During this period he worked with many horses, breaking them in for racing and jumping. There were also many sheep on the property, as well as cattle to be prepared for showing, so there was never a shortage of work to be done.

1948–1951 Dad's time at Bontharambo

Sally Moore, initially a a friend of my sister Carolyn's, but eventually a surrogate family member, became a big part of the Sheather life in 1976. She is a great niece of the Docker brothers and has many memories and stories to tell of her time with our family, including this one relating to the history of Bontharambo itself.

Sally recalls:

> *Jeff worked at Bontharambo as a young farmhand before he was married, training thoroughbreds and working with the stock with my uncle, Stan Docker, his father Hubert Docker and Uncle Geoff Docker. Bontharambo was selected by Reverend Joseph Docker on Reedy Creek, north of the Ovens River in 1838. The Rev. J. Docker took up residence in the bark hut that Faithfull left behind when he came overland from Sydney to Melbourne. Originally Bontharambo comprised of land spreading from the Ovens River to the Murray River—a station to rival any other today, even in Northern Australian terms. The Dockers founded the earliest Angus stud in Australia, bred from Scottish Aberdeen blood. As their wealth increased by selling bullocks to the gold diggers for meat at Beechworth, the Dockers built the existing two-storey sandstone homestead with tower. Perhaps Jeff's time at Bontharambo helped plant a seed to start his own Angus stud later on.*

Dad, Mum, my sisters Mandy and Rita, and I were lucky enough to have the opportunity to visit Bontharambo in 2011, and it was really lovely to hear the way Mary Docker (a granddaughter of one of the Dockers for whom Dad had worked) asked Dad questions about his time there. She asked about several different horses that he trained, but one story seemed to resonate with me: it was about at horse called Hefty Loon.

Dad recalls:

> *The horse that wouldn't jump! He was a bad-tempered horse and didn't particulary like to be ridden. He just wanted to gallop and stopped when you got to the hurdle—yep, a full stop! So with a pair of sharp spurs and slightly modified jumps, we set off. I schooled him over and over and finally got him jumping hurdles, 'cause every time as he tried to stop, he copped the spurs. Once I had him going well, the Dockers decided to send him to Melbourne for training in hurdle racing, with Jack Jury. After he won the*

Grand National, Mrs. Docker bought me a very good camera as a way
of saying thank you for my work with him. They were beautiful people.

In 1951, his first racing season, Hefty Loon won Australia's most prestigious
hurdle race, the Grand National, at fifty-to-one odds. Not a bad effort for a bad-
tempered horse trained by an eighteen-year-old boy.

However, of all the horses that Dad worked with at Bontharambo, it was a mare
called Bonnie that became his pride and joy. He broke her in while he was there
and used her as a stock horse, as they did with all the horses they broke. But
there was something special about her, and they seemed to have a very unique
bond. The photos below were taken two weeks after Dad finished breaking her in,
and it's quite obvious that they trusted each other completely. I cannot imagine
doing those tricks on an older, well-trained horse, let alone one that had just been
broken. To us kids, Dad is the master of all; if he puts his mind to something,
he achieves it. This is part of our legacy: believing in ourselves!

1950: Dad and Bonnie

One of the many stories Dad told us about Bontharambo throughout our
childhood was the story of Nugget falling into the pit. This is the story I have
thought about the most over the years.

Dad recalls:

> *We were digging a pit for a septic tank, which was four feet wide, six feet*
> *long, and six feet deep. We had to chuck the dirt out of the pit, and the*
> *higher you had to throw, the harder the work it was. Stan Docker [Mr.*
> *Hubert's son] and I must have been digging the pit, and Joe Crosier was*

driving a draught horse called Nugget past each side of the pit with a scoop, moving aside the excess dirt.

Nugget had a bugger of a mouth and didn't respond real well, and instead of pulling away from the edge of the pit, he decided he'd go a step further to the right and went ass over the edge! Any rate, I don't remember having any trouble getting out of that pit at all, but Stan was very slow getting out—he was six feet two inches and should have done it easy. He wasn't a very active fellow, though, and as Nugget came in one end, Stan went out the other end.

When he fell in there [I don't know if the photo shows it quite as it was], he had his legs folded up; he'd have laid there quite comfortably but couldn't get up because of his legs. So our very decent square pit, that was very well measured and dug, changed shape. We had to take about two feet off one side all the way down, so Nugget could put his feet out, and then we had to dig a bloody ramp at the far end of the pit to allow him to walk out!

Nugget in the pit

CHAPTER 3

LOVE AND MARRIAGE

Dad left Bontharambo and returned to Trentside approximately three years later to prepare for a trip around Australia with John Barker. Prior to this trip taking place, however, Uncle Murray (Dad's brother) had talked Pop into getting out of beef cattle and into dairying. Then Murray moved away, which unfortunately meant that the trip was not to be. Dad stayed to take over his work, milking the hundred or so dairy cows with Pop on the family farm. It was during this time at Trentside that Dad was to meet his future wife.

In November 1950, Police Constable Jack Toner (Mum's father, known to us as Grandpa) was transferred from Beechworth to Wodonga. Grandpa and Grandma and their seven children, Mum (Patricia), Sally, Peter, Pauline, Kathleen, Danny, and Harry, moved into High Street, Wodonga, and settled into small-town life.

Dad recalls:

> It was some twelve months after Mum arrived in Wodonga, and I had been at a local dance with Brian Dowling, who had been up to Toner's for Sunday lunch. When we were coming past the Rose Maree Café, Brian said, "I know a couple of girls in here," so we went in. Pat and Sally were sitting at a booth having coffee or something, so Brian introduced us, and I'm guessing from here on, we sat down and talked.
>
> That would have been early December, and I wandered up Beechworth Road in the middle of the afternoon a week or so later to see Mum. When her mother opened the door, Pat was standing up on the back of

a lounge chair putting up Christmas decorations. [Mum recalls she had quite a short house dress on at the time.] I asked her if she wanted to go to the pictures or something, and we had our first date before Christmas. We went out that night and continued going out every night afterwards. [Mum pipes up here to say, "That's weekends, not week nights."] I used to get Pop's car to drive on Saturday nights; dates out would be pictures or dancing, and then later on lots of balls were popular. We used to reckon these Catholic balls ought to be cut out 'cause everyone had such bad headaches after them, but they put on good suppers!

1950–1953: Courting

It turns out that Dad had met Grandpa on a few instances prior to all this happening, because the police were responsible for licensing and statistics in those days. Grandpa and Dad soon formed a fast friendship and were known as best mates very early on in the relationship.

Dad and Mum were married approximately eighteen months later on 3 June 1953, and they began their life as Mr. and Mrs. Jeff Sheather at Trentside, where Dad continued to sharefarm with his father for several more years. Ten months after the wedding, Veronica (Roni) Ann was born on 20 April 1954, and then Rosemary (Rosie) Elizabeth was born fourteen months later on 21 June 1955.

3rd June, 1953

1953: The Wedding

It's hard for me to imagine—and even harder for my kids to imagine—but back in those days it flooded for two or three months at a time each year. The floods seemed to have been a part of life back then, and there were times when only the house and the orchard were above water. To get off the property, one had to use a lorry (a large, low wagon without sides, pulled by a draught horse). The safest time to get off the property was when they took the milk cans off to the dairy, because there was enough weight in the drums to keep the lorry anchored, but apparently on the way home the lorry was known to practically float away because the twenty or so drums would be empty. When there were floods, even a trip into town became an adventure. Dad and Mum would pile the milk drums inside a calf crate on the lorry and put planks over the top of that. Then they'd place the kids on top of them and head off. All this just so they could get off the property!

Dad recalls:

> One day I was driving across the water, when the horse went one way and we all went the other way, just floating downstream. We had times when the only place we could feed hay was in the orchard, due to the floods. Over three hundred acres of land would be underwater for two or three months a year, and only one small area around the house was dry! The cows got so hungry they were known to eat the nappies from the clothes line.

For as long as I can remember, Dad has talked about the floods, as well as the time he and his horse Frosty nearly drowned. There was a newspaper article written about this event in the local newsapaer, the *Border Morning Mail*, which was titled "Shades of Robinson Crusoe." I believe the year was 1956, and this is Dad's recollection of that day.

> We had to go across a big stream to get to the horses that were on the other side of the island. I told the fellow that was working with me to wait there and I gave him the shotgun. I was carrying a shotgun at the time for shooting hares, rabbits, and snakes. I said, "Hang onto the thing, and I'll go across and get these horses."
>
> I'd been in the water for eight or nine hours by this stage, and when we started swimming across, my horse Frosty, who had been swimming along like a champ, just cramped up. The wet saddle was probably the

cause, but it wasn't until the water came up around my waist, and then up around over my shoulders, that I knew I was in trouble. The horse wasn't moving as his legs had cramped. He was a big horse, and with his hindquarters being the heaviest, they just hung down; all that was sticking out was about six inches of his nose. Then it was over his eyes, and all that I had to hang onto was his mane, and we were floating well down the stream. I tried to go higher up his neck, to get my head out of the water further, and then all of a sudden instead of trying to pull myself up, I pulled him over backwards.

He was just like a ball in the water, just floating. I was able to kick and push and got him leaning forward again, and then I put my hands down into the water and held onto his mane at his withers, right down low on his neck, so it didn't alter his balance. I knew we were going to go over a fence, and knowing that it would have been about eight or nine feet from the tip of Frosty's nose to where his feet would have been hanging in the water, I thought, "Shit, what's going to happen when we hit this fence?" but evidently it had been washed away or we floated over the top of it, which was a great relief.

Then I remembered the creek. It was a big one that took a fairly sharp bend, and there were sucker trees fifteen feet high on the edge of the bank with debris washed onto them; it was the closest we had got to land or anything that looked like it. It's amazing what you think about at times like these, as I thought, "This would be a great place for snakes to lie on this, out in the sun", and "I'm leaving you Frosty old boy".

I was able to push myself far enough away to get my arms above where I thought any snakes might be, and I got on top for a bit and thought, I can't stay here. Within about six feet I could see some rushes which I knew would have solid ground under them, and I thought I could swim across that six feet, but there was no bloody hope. Dressed in gumboots, moleskins, cartridge belt, and woolen shirt, all saturated, I got as much spring off the trees as I could, and in that six feet, by the time I got to the bank the sucker trees were hanging straight down, and it was a toss-up whether my arms got onto dirt or my feet kicked the bank first.

At any rate, I crawled up onto the bank, walked out of the water, and found a dry spot. I got my cigarette lighter out and took the cotton wool from inside it, to sit it on a limb in a bit of sun and wind to dry out; I did the same thing with the flint. This was over a period of about three or four hours, and then I lit myself a fire by putting the dry flint on the cotton wool. The man that I'd left waiting had got worried and went to Wodonga to get the police. Pat's dad was one of the police who came down in the rescue boat, and when the they turned up, I was sitting there beside a fire trying to dry out. I could hear Frosty groaning from about a mile downstream.

When the police came they were going to take me home, and I said, "I'm not going home. I'm going to get my horse." Once again, somewhere along the way the creek had turned like buggery, and where the water went out over the ground, it must have only been deep enough that it washed him out, and he ended up only about fifty or sixty yards from the main stream. I don't know how he kept his head out of the water because he was lying on his side. I could hear a lot of grunting and groaning coming from downstream, but about half an hour later he was standing up.

In the meantime, Mum was waiting for him to come home for afternoon tea, but he recalls that he didn't get home until around seven at night. She says she wasn't worried but was angry, because he was supposed to be home to milk the cows, and she wasn't going to do it, as she was seven or eight months pregnant at the time. When he opened the door, she apparently said something along the lines of, "Where the hell have you been?"

He replied, "Can't you see I've got different clothes on?" as if that would explain everything.

image by Carolyn Sheather

CHAPTER 4

THE ROAD TO INDEPENDENCE

With baby number three on the way, Dad and Mum thought they had better get off the flooded property before the birth, because they thought it might be a bit difficult to get out in the middle of the night if the need arose. They packed up the calf crate with the planks, to head off to stay in Wodonga with Grandma and Grandpa, but even that wasn't easy. They decided that they should take what groceries they had, so they packed them into suitcases. While they were getting the two kids organised, one of the sows decided to rip into one of the suitcases and help herself to the food.

1956: Trentside Floods

Such was life for about a month, with Dad travelling back and forth between Wodonga and Trentside until Helen Maree was born on 13 September 1956 and

Mum was ready to return back to the farm. They put up with hardships like that for the first three years of their married life, and when Helen was three weeks old, they decided to move to South Australia.

Cookie, now married to Dad's sister Nita, had invited Dad and Mum over for a holiday. This holiday was to be the catalyst for a change of location and the start of what was going to be an independent life for them.

Dad recalls:

> In 1955 when Rosie was just a baby and Cookie was sharefarming dairy cows in Mount Compass, South Australia, he said, "Come on over for a holiday," and so we did. Cookie had said to his neighbour Bob Shepherd, "I've got a fellow that can swim the Murray River, do this and that," and then one day when Bob had got his tractor bogged in a dirty, great dam Cookie says, "This fellow can do it—he'll get it out." Meanwhile, Mum's at home waiting for dinner with two kids with measles, and I'm running two hours late. But I finally found the tractor, diving down in underwear only and standing on the steering wheel so I could breathe. We eventually managed to tie a cable to the back of it and pull it out.

Not long afterwards, Bob Shepard, tired of Cookie's stories, relented and employed Dad on a commission basis for just over thirteen months. His property was known as Tallara, and he ran stud Angus cattle and South Down sheep. On arrival Dad and Mum lived in a small tin house that had nothing in it but a stove, as there was no other accommodation for them on the property. Fortunately this was only for three weeks, and then they moved into a proper house on the property when it became vacant.

Dad recalls:

> Helen was three weeks old, and the house we moved into at Myponga, South Australia, wasn't much more than a shack—iron inside and out, and a stove in the kitchen was the only fitting. In those days there was no power, and it was cold. It was a six-hundred-mile trip, and we had bought a new Land Rover and built a trailer to head to South Australia.

We had the Land Rover and trailer loaded to the hilt, and then I thought, "Where am I going to put my chooks?" So I made a crate to go on the triangle at the front of the trailer, and the dog went there, too.

We left Wodonga at three o'clock in the afternoon, and at Winton we got a flat tyre. We took the spare tyre into Benalla and then stayed the night in the Land Rover with the three kids. The suitcases were packed into the back seat with a mattress on top, for the kids to sleep on the way. The thing we made the canopy on the trailer out of sat in the back yard for some time when we got over there. There were no cupboards in the house, so I built two sets of kitchen cupboards out of the canopy, the only masonite we had. These were the cupboards that were in all our houses up to Kiewa, and then Brenda and Neale took them.

1957: Roni, Rosie, and Helen at Myponga

Dad has fond memories of working for Bob Shepard while they lived in South Australia, and Bob also recalls some of their times together with much affection and laughter.

Bob recalls:

Your Dad did get into strife up on our hills block one day. He had the super spreader on behind him, and he thought he could get around this side; it was stick country. The tractor slipped down the hill, so he walked to Hillsley Station and rang me from there, and he said, "You better drive it out." I said, "You put it there, you better drive it out." But I went on out, and I unhooked the super spreader and let it slide on down the hill. Then we got the tractor out, and then got the super spreader out as well.

One hot day we went up to the hills block to dip the sheep. We both had a thermos, and I said, "If we are out of this damn place by one o'clock, I'm going to the Pub," because we were on the old coach way, nearby to our top block. When we got them through the dip, we headed on down to the pub. On the way down I said, "Have you got any money, Jeff?" He said, "About enough to buy a butcher of beer." I said, "Well, that's about all I've got." Jeff said, "How are we going to get on then?" I said, "Leave it to me." You can imagine what we looked like, covered in dust and perspiration, but there used to be a big old tank at the pub, so we had a bit of a wash-up before heading into the pub.

When we walked in, there was only one other chap there. The chap that owned the pub wasn't there; instead there was a total stranger behind the bar, and I ordered two pints, being the biggest item you could order. He brought them down and put them in front of us, and I said "Can you give us a pound out of the till?" He said, "What? Do you know Bert [the owner of the pub]? You must know Bert really well!" There was another chap from Myponga at the bar, drinking on his own, and the publican says to him, "Do you know these two fellows at the top of the bar?" He looks at us and says, "Yeah, I know them," so the publican brought us over our pound. When Bert came back later, the publican says to him quietly, "I gave them a quid." Old Bert says, "I reckon they could do with another one! Throw another one down the bar!"

I would imagine it was with a certain amount of regret that a short time after having settled into life at Myponga, Dad and Mum would embark on yet another move. On 8 October 1957, Carolyn Patricia was born, and six weeks after her birth Mum contracted pulmonary tuberculosis, or 'TB' as it is more commonly known. In November, they made a trip back to Wodonga to catch up with family, and when Mum sought medical advice for her condition, she was told she would need to be hospitalised for an extended period of time. They headed back to South Australia to pack the necessities and temporarily move back to Wodonga. Mum ended up in hosptial for around six months, and whilst she was there, Roni and Rosie went to stay with Aunty Sylvia, Helen stayed with Aunty Joy (Jocelyn), and Carolyn stayed with Grandma and Grandpa (Mum's parents). Dad headed back to South Australia with Mum's younger brother Harry, to pack up their belongings and bring everything home to Wodonga, where he then rented a house in Vermont Street.

Dad recalls:

> We had a Vanguard that we took the backseat out of and then stripped off as much as we could. Once we got everything packed in Myponda, we put everything but the breakables in the Vanguard; everything else we put on rail freight. The night before leaving, I had a few drinks. I remember running around at two or three in the morning trying to get everyone to go home, but mates kept coming around, and Harry kept saying, "Enjoy yourself! I'll keep you awake on the way home."
>
> The next morning we get into the trip home only to find the back end of the Vanguard is way too heavy—the front wheels are off the ground. By 9:00 AM Harry is sound asleep. We left at sunrise and arrived in Wodonga at around 1:30 AM the following morning. Harry had woken a few times only to be abused, and then he'd go back to sleep. When we finally made it back home, the only door that was unlocked was the laundry door, so we slept in there on the floor so that we wouldn't wake anyone.

It turns out that with the short amount of notice Dad was able to give in Myponga, Bob didn't have the money to pay the commission and wages Dad was owed, so in lieu of payment he gave Dad four stud Angus cows and one young bull. The cattle were shipped back to Victoria by train, and Dad kept Vicki, one of the cows, in the back yard to milk. The other cattle were moved around from place to place in town—anywhere Dad could find feed for them, such as the saleyards or makeshift paddocks by the railway line.

Whilst Mum was in hospital, Dad had three different jobs. During the week he worked on the railway line at Wodonga Flats as a carpenter and labourer; he had no qualifications, but given that he was pretty handy and had some tools and a truck, he found work. He would sometimes take five other workers in his truck out to Wodonga Flats and charge them one pound each for the privilege. His second job was as a sewer system employee. At 3:00 AM on Saturday mornings he would go out to Bethanga and exchange empty toilet cans for clean ones, and then he'd dispose of the waste out at the sewerage farm, where it was buried. He would then go on to Tallangatta to commence his third job, the weekly garbage run, after he stopped for breakfast (generally a Fritz and tomato sauce sandwich by the side of the road). He would be finished by lunchtime and head home for a shower. Then he'd be off to the local footy ground, grab a pie, and watch the game.

During the course of Mum's hospitalisation, she had a night at home after her grandmother's funeral. Although it was a sad occasion, it was also the only time she spent at home with her family in the six-month period. It was on this one and only home visit that another child was conceived, and on 9 Januray 1959, their first son, Jeffery John, was born.

Unfortunately, when Jeffery was only two months old, Mum had relapsed and was hospitalised with TB, and so once again the children were sent to stay with different relatives so that Dad could continue to work. It was while Mum was in hospital the second time (only for six weeks this stint) that Dad decided to stick a halter on Vicki and lead her up to the show grounds to see how she would perform in the Angus section at the Wodonga Show. It turned out that she did quite well, and this led to Dad being offered a grooming position with Bill Goode of Glenelg Angus Stud in Culcairn. The condition of Dad accepting this offer from Bill was that he could take his four cows to breed with, but he sold his bull at the market. Bill accepted this condition, and they started a share-farming arrangement. Dad was one to find a way to make some extra money on the side, and he talked Bill into building a dairy for extra income, with Dad purchasing some twenty milking cows and Bill paying for the dairy to be built. Dad continued grooming and working the show circuit with Bill and every day he milked the cows morning and night.

Dad recalls:

> Bill Goode, from Glenelg Angus Stud, was there with his team for the Sydney Show, and Vicki won champion cow over Glenelg. This didn't make Bill very happy, but he realised that if he wanted me to come and work for him, he would have to play ball—which meant if I went, the cattle had to come with me. I took the four cows and left the bull, because I would have use of Glenelg bulls. Mother was told she could come out of

hospital if she could live in a drier climate, and you don't get much drier than Culcairn.

Dad and Mum stayed at Culcairn for close to two years, and in this time their second son, Gregory Clifford (Cliff), was born on 8 May 1960. During this time at Culcairn, Dad began his breeding program, and Coomooroo Angus was registered as a stud name. He continued to show his cattle at the local shows while slowly establishing his name in the industry. It was while Dad was working at Culcairn that he met Max Doherty of Tulagi Angus Stud in Deniliquin, and Dad started doing some show grooming with him as well.

Greg Doherty, Max's son, recalls:

> *Max and Jeff would have started showing together in the early '60s, and from there your Dad became a show groom for him. Melbourne Show was a three- or four-week enterprise, and Sydney was a four- to five-week adventure. It began with loading the Talagi cattle onto the train in Finley and picking up Jeff and his team on the way. The trip took about twenty-four hours to Sydney, and they had a ball. I never did the train run—they wouldn't let me! [Greg was only eighteen at this stage.] Max couldn't be away from the property for these periods of time, so that's why Jeff became show groom for him at the Royals.*

CHAPTER 5

A HOME OF THEIR OWN

Sometime in 1960, one of Bill Goode's neighbours, Arthur King, asked Dad why he was working for Bill instead of running his own property. Dad said that with six kids and not much in the bank, he wasn't likely to be able to afford a property of his own. The neighbour offered to lend Dad and Mum the deposit if they could find a property that suited them. Let me tell you, they didn't waste any time in finding that property!

It was from this gentleman's generousity that Coomooroo Angus Stud was born, in May 1961, on a 110-acre property purchased from George Dickson at Cheshunt, Victoria. Upon leaving Glenelg, Dad took with him his breeding stock from South Australia, the dairy cows and an Angus calf that had adopted one of Dad's cows as its mother. They also purchased the cattle that George Dickson had been milking on the property.

1961–1971: Home and Cattle

Dad and Mum continued to milk dairy cows, which was their main source of income, but Dad also did a calf run on Sundays. Sometimes he would sell all the calves on the same day, but on other days he would have to take them up to Wodonga during the week to sell them at the sale yards. They also had sheep, pigs, and chooks on the farm as well, and with bread and butter being delivered with the mail, they managed to be quite self-sufficient. As the stud numbers grew, the breeding and showing became more predominent than the milking, until they eventually sold the majority of the dairy cattle and focused soley on the Angus.

Dad recalls:

> *One of the dairy cows, Lucy, was a foster mother to Cavalier, an Angus bull calf that we'd bred while we were at Culcairn. When we left, I ended up taking Lucy and the calf, and at two years of age he was still suckling from her! Coomooroo Cavalier went onto become the first Coomooroo working stud sire.*

It was during these early days in Cheshunt that Dad and Mum formed lifetime friendships with many of the locals. The O'Donoghues, the Pizzinis, Keith and Pat Rooks, and Harvey Haigh come to mind when I think back to my early childhood in Cheshunt. I have thoroughly enjoyed contacting these people and hearing or reading the wonderful things they have to say about my parents. This is what Uncle Dan (Dan O'Donoghue, no relation) had to say about Dad.

> *He is a remarkable man. He left school when he was fourteen and went to work at Bontharambo, and for the rest of his life, it didn't matter what he undertook—whether it was life, stock, or farming, he mastered every craft. Not only that, but he could mix in any company. They brought a show judge out from Scotland, a world-famous judge, and your father could sit down and talk to him the same as I'm talking to you. When he was at Bontharambo, they had a string of racehorses that your father broke. I don't know where he went from Bontharambo, or how old he was when he got there; I don't know anything about that until he got to Cheshunt.*

> *He had no capital, but he had one asset more than anyone else had, and that was your mother. He was self-educated. He was a smart man, and not just the basics—he could talk on any subject.*

> *Do you remember the little white pony we had? I bought a little white foal; it was a welsh mountain pony, and he broke it in. He brought it over and said, "The kids can ride it." I said, "Who's ridden it before?" He replied,*

"No one, but it'll be all right." And it was! He was a horse whisperer, but he was better at cattle.

I remember Max Doherty said to me one night, "Do you think Jeff would look after my cattle at the Sydney Show?" I said, "You've only got to ask him." So he did, and Max won three championships and reserve championships at that show. That was the year the Scottish judge came out, and he complimented Max on the way his cattle were prepared. Max just pointed to Jeff.

He [Dad] judged all over the eastern states, and I'm pretty sure he judged at Royal Shows, too. He could see something at a glance that would take other people a week to notice; he just had to look, and he could see. He was widely recognised as a superb judge of cattle and a great breeder of cattle, too. He was absolutely remarkable! He reared you kids on a shoestring, and you all did well. Not only that, but he was involved in public life: school committee, hall committee, fire brigade. I don't know how he found the time.

One of his most remarkable feats was when he drove the Plymouth for eighteen months without a reverse gear! He would pull a trailer and took pigs to the market, and then he'd say, "Give us a hand to push it back, would you?" They [Dad and Mum] used to go to Wangaratta once a week and park, obviously parallel, and he'd park it next to a driveway so he could just drive out again. Nothing was a trouble to him, and he'd do anything for you.

It was early in the sixties when they moved to Cheshunt, but I have no clear recollection of when or where we met. We used to do our hay together; I'd bale his hay, and then he'd come over to my place and help me cart mine.

He left every place twice as good as when he bought it—pasture, fencing, everything. Twice as good, if not better! And he did it on no budget. [I suggested here that it might have had something to do with all the children helping, but Uncle Dan didn't necessarily agree.] I never heard him say a cross word. Always with a smile on his face that would stop a train! All *of our kids thought the world of him; they didn't take any notice of what I said, but they'd listen to him.*

He was absolutely remarkable, and he stood out. Remarkable! As I said, only a basic education, went to work when he was fourteen, finished up with a beautiful house and car, and judged a Sydney show. There's not many people who have done that! But don't forget your mother's part in all that, either. She was computer wise, she could keep stud records, and no doubt she passed on a lot of knowledge to him. But look, you only had to blink, and he'd pick it up and never forget. He had a very acute mind and could pick up anything at a glance.

One of his best achievements was a day when he was judging cattle at the Tallangatta Show. I drove us to the show, and we had to walk up a hill to the judging ring. A group of local breeders had purchased a very expensive bull for Doug Blair, and he was in the senior bull class. Your father put him last in the class. Well!, when we got down to the bar to have a beer, Doug said, "What the hell did you do that for?" Your Dad said, "He has a white patch under his belly," which he had spotted while walking up the hill to get to the ring earlier on. No one else had seen it.

Val and George Pizzini were a big part of our life in Cheshunt, and Dad showed George how the show circuit worked when he started a Murray Grey stud. They continued to work together for many years, Mum and Val became great friends, and we always had a great time when we got together as families.

Val recalls:

I can't remember what year we met Jeff, Pat, and the family, but George met Jeff, and I guess it was something to do with cattle. He came home one day and said we were invited up for dinner on Saturday night with our family [Gary, Linda, Debbie, and David]. We had a lovely meal, and we thought what a great person Pat is, having six extra for dinner on top of their large family. After dinner the children cleared the table and did the dishes, and then the girls played music and the boys played cricket. George and Jeff settled in to talk cattle, and I got to know Pat. That started a lovely friendship, and we went up to their place many times, playing cards or just chatting.

We had just started our Murray Grey stud and didn't know much about showing, so Jeff asked George to go to Melbourne show with him for the ten days, to learn about show cattle—about grooming them and leading them. Jeff was the best in the business, and he knew cattle inside and out. George couldn't have had a better teacher, and he came home saying Jeff had taught him a lot.

Jeff was well liked with all the cattle people. I can remember going around all the country shows where we would meet up with Jeff and Pat; they were good times. Jeff would come up and help George to trim the feet of the cattle, and he was always ready to give some tips. Once we had a Murray Grey sale on our property, and Jeff was the ring master; he did a wonderful job as he always did. He was the master of cattle and loved what he was doing.

The seventh Sheather child was born three months after the move to Cheshunt. Susan Lynne (that's me) was born by Cesarean section on 14 August 1961, with the doctors telling Mum that there should be no more children after such a difficult birth. Thirteen months later, however, Mum was pregnant again, and though the pregnancy and birth went well, Amanda Joy (Mandy) was born on 3 June 1963 with a harelip. At three months of age Mandy went to Melbourne for plastic surgery, with Grandma taking care of her while Dad and Mum stayed in Cheshunt with the rest of the children. In the following three years, three more children were born: Rita Mary on 2 July 1964, Brenda Louise on 20 August 1965, and Paul Anthony (Fred) on 25 November 1966. The doctors said she *shouldn't* have more children—not that she couldn't.

As kids we all have the fondest memories of Cheshunt. It truly was a wonderful life, full of hard work because Dad always had us picking up stones out of the paddocks, or helping to paint all the fence posts white, or pulling out every weed on the property. Boy, did he know how to make a place look great—and let's face it, with all the kids they had, he had the hands to make it happen. I remember it used to seem like such hard, unfair work, being out in the paddock in the hot sun, having to pick up stupid sticks or stones, or doing whatever the work he instructed on that particular day, but every evening we would laugh and muck about.

Dad was always a hard task master during the day, but he was the best of fun in the evenings, or when he took some down time with us. We used to have a small above-ground swimming pool that was probably about six feet round, and it was the best thing when Dad got in with us. We would all pile around him and splash and have the best time. He was the best Dad in the world, and he still is.

1963–1969: Family at Cheshunt

I don't remember ever having that sort of fun and frivolity with Mum, but I do remember she always cooked the best food, and there was always so much of it. She was the bedrock of the family, and I'm sure it was her constant love and attention to detail that kept everything together. She made our clothes and did all the washing in an old drum machine where she had to manually feed the clothes through the wringer. She always made us a birthday cake and made the day as special as it could be. Though we may not have had a lot materially, it was more than made up for with love and happiness.

Harvey Haigh has been a friend of our family for most of my life, and these are some of his memories.

I first met Jeff and Pat with Johnny Lewis [Johnny was Mum's brother in law at the time and he was also a member of the Police Force where he and Harvey became friends] *in 1962. We got to Cheshunt, and Jeff went out driving us around all night spot lighting. The next morning he was up at five o'clock milking cows, while John was having a wonderful time sleeping in until 10:00 AM. I could only do that one day, and I thought, "He's out all night driving us around, and no one's helping him early in the day, and that's wrong." And so the next day I was up at 5:00 AM. Didn't know shit from clay, and I was running after cows*

34

and trying to do the things he was showing me how to do. I couldn't milk a cow, but Jeff had great delight trying to get me to do it.

I then started to make a regular thing of it—not to go spotlighting, but to go up and catch up with these two people and their kids. I thoroughly enjoyed the family and their lives. You [Sue] were the baby when I met the family, and I remember Mandy coming into the world. Life was a struggle for your folks in those days; they had this big family, and Jeff was working his arse off, stubbing his toes every now and then, and not quite reaching the heights he wanted. It worked out that when I went there, I always took a big box of groceries and dumped them on the table, 'cause they always looked after me, and I couldn't go with nothing. I tried to pay my way.

As time went by, we did a lot of fencing. We had a tractor and a trailer, and we went up behind Smalls' place [next-door neighbours] to cut trees down for posts. We had wedges and sledgehammers to cut them up, we'd split them all, and then we'd go down and dig the holes we had to brace them in, and put through all the wires and things.

Eventually it worked out that Jeff was helping Max Doherty as a groom for Sydney Show and then Melbourne Show. I'd take my annual leave then, to go up to Cheshunt and help run the farm while Jeff was away. I would do the harrowing and whatever needed to be done.

Within a few short years of buying the Cheshunt property, the stud had grown to sixty-five head of cattle. This was a herd size that Dad tried to maintain, because he believed that a good stud was about quality and not quantity. Five years after establishing Coomooroo Angus Stud, he had his first reduction sale to keep numbers at this size.

Up until this point Dad had only exhibited cattle at country shows. It wasn't until 1966 that he started showing at the Royals and was judging at the country shows by 1968. With championships being won by Coomooroo Angus at both Sydney and Melbourne Royal Shows, everyone within the industry knew that a real player was here to stay.

All that Dad and Mum had achieved up to this point in the growth of the stud—the reknown, the respect, and the rewards—these were just stepping stones in the growth that had taken place since the purchase of the property ten years prior. In June 1971 Dad entered eight stud bulls for sale at the Dalgety Wangaratta Bull Sale partly to reduce his numbers (which now stood at 159 stud cattle) but also because he realised that they had outgrown their Cheshunt property.

At the Sydney Royal Show in 1971, Dad, along with Max and Greg Doherty, were presented championship ribbons by the Duke of Edinburgh. Glenelg Luke, one of Dad's bulls, had won reserve junior champion, and we were all so proud of him. How many kids got to say their dad had shaken hands with the king of England? (That was my perspective of it back then.) It was such a big deal, and photos were in all of the newspapers. We all thought Dad was famous!

1971 – Sydney Royal Show

Fred Wyatt recalls:

> *I remember the time when Jeff and Greg Doherty shook the hand of Prince Phillip in the judging ring after winning junior champion. Later in the day they won a trophy for a pair of bulls, or a bull and a heifer, and we went out for a tasty meal at some fancy restaurant in Sydney. They celebrated all that night, and the following morning they were missing! They hadn't mucked their cattle out, and it was time for the tractor to come through to get the soiled straw, so a mate and I did it for them. I think there would have been about fifteen to eighteen head of cattle, and we put down two bales of straw, which we thought wasn't much for that many cattle. When they came in, your dad roars, "Who did this?" With chest out, I said, "I did." There was no thank-you, just a response of, "That's too much. I'd of only put down one." We still often talk and laugh about that.*

They had some excellent breeding stock by this stage, with Coomooroo Karen being their most prized cow of all: she seemed to win championships wherever she went. Vixen, Minx, and Nola were also winning their fair share of prizes and were excellent breeders.

Greg Doherty recalls a Melbourne Show with Coomooroo Karen.

About three days before judging, I was in the shed spreading straw, and I put the pitchfork down to get some more straw but ended up putting the fork between Karen's toes. "Aw shit!" I was the worst bloke in the world, but we had to get her better and ready for the show. I felt so bad. Jeff could have torn strips off me, but he didn't. He took it all in stride and got on with things. Plenty of cream was applied, and three days later she was fine and ready to show. She was a bloody good cow, that one; I think she even went on to take out champion cow.

CHAPTER 6
DREAMS BECOME REALITY

In November 1971 Dad and Mum moved from Cheshunt to a eighty-hectare property at Markwood, twelve miles from Wangaratta. This property had fallen into a state of disrepair. As one of the original homesteads in the area and formerly the local garage, it needed a lot of work, and like Cheshunt they made many improvements and turned it into an oustanding property during their stay there.

The Markwood Homestead

I recall:

> I remember that next to the house there was an old, overgrown orchard. Dad soon got to that and took out everything that wasn't productive. The kids all got in there as well and did the weeding, and Mum created a vegetable garden down the back, with flower beds in the front yard and down the other side of the house. The house was painted inside and out, a white picket fence was restored at the front of the house yard, and bird aviaries and ferneries were built. Dad went about building new fences and painting fence posts white,

all the while getting us to pick up every stick and stone on the property. It really was an amazing-looking property by the time they had finished.

In 1972 Dad sold ten stud bulls at the Wodonga Angus Sale, and he sold his top sire at the time, Glenelg Luke, for a South Australian record price of six thousand dollars. He continued showing around the state and attending Sydney and Melbourne Royal Shows, all the while evolving in the industry as a serious breeder of Angus cattle.

In 1973 changes were happening for both the family and the stud. The children were growing up and getting married, the cattle numbers had now reached 180 head, and Dad's reputation was rock solid. This was probably the most pivotal and important year of Dad's show career because it was the year his name was concreted into Angus history in Australia.

This was the year he sold one of his junior bulls, Coomooroo Q-Crusader (seventeen months old), for an Australian record junior Angus bull price of eleven thousand dollars to the Ben Nevis Angus Stud in New South Wales. Bruce Steel, the owner of Ben Nevis, told Dad that he had been coming to the Sydney Show for 22 years and this was the first bull he had seen that he was not going to go home without. As part of the sale agreement Dad retained 300 straws of semen, which equated to a 1/4 share of the value of Crusader and this led, in part, to the outstanding success that was achieved by the Stud in 1978.

He then went on to sell another junior bull, Coomooroo Revenue (six months old), to the Romsey Kahlua Stud for an Australian record Angus calf price of three thousand dollars. Coomooroo Karen was the mother of both these bulls, and Dad was offered yet another record price of six thousand for her at around the same time. But given that she was in calf again, he decided to take a gamble on her progeny, which paid off nicely because he later sold the calf on its own for five thousand dollars. Karen went on to win championships and produce more champion progeny for several more years. The story of these record prices was in every newspaper nationwide, and once again Dad was famous to his eleven children. We thought Dad and Mum must have been filthy rich, to have sold cattle for that much money!

★COOMOOROO★
BREEDS
—SUPREME ANGUS—

★ COOMOOROO-Q-CRUSADER — Sold 1973 for Australian Record Junior Angus Bull Price $11,000
★ COOMOOROO REVENUE — Sold 1973 for Australian Record Angus Calf Price of $3,000
★ GLENELG LUKE — Sold 1972 to Uganda Stud, S.A. for Top S. A. Angus Purchase Price of $6,000

"COOMOOROO - Q - CRUSADER" — Junior Champion, 1973 Sydney Royal Show with Jeff Sheather (breeder—left) and buyers, Mr. and Mrs. Bruce Steele, who paid $11,000.

1971-1973 Record Breakers

It was also in 1973 that Dad started winning Angus Carcass Classes at both Royal and Country Shows. At this stage of their show career, Coomooroo Cattle had amassed an amazing amount of wins.

- 24 interbreed championships
- 16 supreme Angus rosettes
- 44 championships
- 18 reserve championships
- 124 first prizes
- 58 second prizes
- A total of 73 trophies

In 1973 alone, the stud won seven interbreed championships, seven rosettes, twenty-nine championships, and fifty-one first places. Though we were in awe of all Dad and Mum had achieved, apparently it's not all hard work at the Royal Shows, as all who remember will happily tell.

James Tubb was known as Tubby, and he has known Dad and Mum since the 1968 Melbourne Show.

Tubby recalls:,

> We had some great times at the Royal Shows, and lots of fun! But it wasn't all fun—we had a lot of work to do. Get up early, work all day, and have some fun at night. JC [Dad] was the boss. We went to the shows for six years in a row, and I looked forward to meeting up with JC each time. In those days the show didn't open on Easter Sunday—everything was very quite that day—and JC always felt very lonely and was very quiet because he was missing his family [he had already been away for three weeks by then].
>
> We would leave Finley at seven Friday night by train, and we'd get to Sydney at two on Saturday morning—very tired. At the old show ground it was very rough living quarters. JC and I slept in the cattle huts with not much room, and JC snored and made other noises all night. I thought, Poor Pat!

Others remember the shows more as fun than work. Fred Wyatt recalls:

> There was the time Jeff had been kicking the football on the judging lawns outside the bull shed, and as you can imagine, he got pretty sweaty. Well, he was just lying on his back resting, and I was there with him talking, and I just started to wrestle with him. I could not hold him because he was so sweaty and slippery, and then all of a sudden he just grabbed me, rolled me in a ball, and flick! I was gone. It hurt! The next morning I went to the Red Cross station, and they just told me not to fight bigger men than myself, which I had already worked out. On getting home I went to the doctor, and he told me I had one slightly cracked rib. Ouch!
>
> Another time, you couldn't buy beer on Good Friday, so Jeff had a big fridge in his locker, and we would fill it up with beer the day before, with

no room for food. On Good Friday you would have to fight the crowd to get near enough to open the locker door to get a beer. Smoke would waft out, and you would step over bodies to get close to it, and you would end up with a very high-pitched voice after the wrestle to get out!

And then there is this recollection from Greg Doherty:

I used to sleep in the same block as Jeff at the Royal Shows; boy, was he funny. He checked his undies each morning to see if he could get another wear out of them, and he used to say, "Always wear your thongs in the shower." I was about eighteen when I started, and I didn't drink, but those boys sure taught me—though they didn't teach me very well. I remember we used to go the pub after doing all our work in the shed in the mornings, and then we would go back down the hill for the afternoon parade.

This is what we would do. You were that buggered in Sydney, walking around on concrete all of the time. You'd be up at five in the morning to get everything finished by seven, have your breakfast, and get showered. We used to put different ribbons on different cattle each day to go out in the parade to give them all a turn for a walk, and we'd all be half pissed. The cattle just knew it; they would walk us around the ring. Of course we'd feed up in the afternoon, and then we'd go and have another beer. You were leg weary all the time, and you would come home again for a holiday 'cause you were stuffed.

In 1974 Dad judged at the Adelaide Show, after having sold forty-eight cows and heifers to six studs in four different states. The word was out, and both the stock produced by Coomooroo and the keen mind of Jeff Sheather were sought after Australia wide. His show achievements for the Royal Shows for the year included:

- Senior champion Bull
- Reserve senior champion Bull
- Two reserve junior champion females
- Seven first places, as well as a second place and a third place

As his reputation grew, so did the demand for his advice on breeding and showing for all cattle breeds around the country. Somehow he managed to travel quite extensively in an advisory capacity whilst still breeding and showing his own stock and caring for the family and farm.

1975: Theme, Sterling, and Sargeant

The major achievement for 1975 was Coomooroo Sargeant being awarded the highest points in the Victorian Section of National Beef Sire of the Year Award, and he was also third nationally. This was a huge achievement because this is a competition over all beef breeds Australia wide. Sargeant was the bull of the year for Coomooroo, seemingly winning wherever he was shown. The judge at the Melbourne Royal Show actually said he was "very close to the ideal Angus bull, with excellent fleshing in all the right places." He was sold during the year to the same stud that had purchased Q-Crusader two years earlier. All round it was an extremely successful show year for Coomooroo, with excellent results at both the Royal and Country Shows.

Dad and another breeder, Eric Moyle, created the concept of the Wodonga National Show and Sale, which was then established in 1977. Dad was also instrumental in forming the North Eastern Riverina Angus Breeders Group. He was never shy when it came to getting involved in promoting the awareness of Angus cattle and exposing them to more buyers.

In 1978 Dad was electrocuted whilst fighting a fire at the entrance to one of the paddocks at the Markwood property. Dad recalls there was a man grading the side of the road down one side of the property, Morris Lane, when he saw smoke. He grabbed his knapsack and asked Mum to call the fire brigade and send Cliff up to help him. Dad and Cliff have different versions of what happened, but at the end of the day, Dad was electrocuted. Fortunately the SEC were out at the front of the property at the time and were able to contain the electricity outage quite quickly.

Cliff recalls:

> Dad grabbed his knapsack and rode the motorbike down to the fire, and I was to grab a hessian bag—because we didn't have two knapsacks—and follow him on the other bike. So I headed down there, and I remember I was belting away at the bloody fire with a bag, and the grader driver (he'd been into the paddock and driven around the fire to cut a break with the blade) came up to the other side of the fence. We were still on the road side, and he said to me "Watch out! The power line is down. Go and tell your dad."
>
> So I raced up and told Dad, but I don't recall him ever getting the message clear. Oh well! He got the message, but he didn't comprehend where the power line was. It was down at face height—to me, that is—and as I turned around and headed away after I told him, he just went straight into it, walked into it. I remember seeing the blue arc on the side of his face. I think I was still watching him as I was walking away, because I still wasn't sure that he knew exactly where the power line was. Anyway, he walked in to it, and it threw him back a couple of metres. Might have been three or four metres to the road from the fence, so it bloody whacked him hard! He still had on the metal knapsack, and he pretty much landed on it and everything else.
>
> He just got up, not too gingerly or anything, and got back to putting the fire out. I really don't know if I helped him get up or not, but once I knew he was and up going, well, I just went back to the other end of the fire where I was working. He didn't stop until the fire was under control.

The fire truck soon arrived and took care of the clean-up, and Dad was taken to the doctors for a check-up. Though the doctors recommended he be hospitalised, he refused and came home again, even though it was believed he had fused a few vertebra together. For the next twelve months the Country Fire Authority paid Dad a wage while he recovered to some extent. Though he still showed cattle throughout the year, his back caused him a lot of grief and definitely slowed him down.

This may have been one of the reasons that our family friend, Sally Moore was asked to start showing with the family. Another set of keen hands was always appreciated, and Dad's recovery was always going to be a long, slow one.

Sally recalls:

> *Jeff first asked me to help prepare and show his Angus show team for the Royal Melbourne Show in 1977. Jeff, Cliff, and Carole taught me about showing cattle, from how to shampoo, blow up [blow-dryer with a crevice tool], groom, and lead cattle to show off their best features for the judge. Jeff proudly won grand champion bull and cow that year, after many nervously smoked cigarettes. Jeff and Cliff taught the show team to lead by encouragement, brute strength, and willpower, but if all else failed, behind the Ford tractor. Later on [following the move to Glenrowan] it was found to be easier to tie them up to a Jenny [female donkey] for a couple of days; this took all the hard work out of training cattle to lead.*
>
> *To ensure the cattle walked smartly around the show ring, you could often hear Jeff pretend to whistle up Dodger, his trusty Queensland heeler. Dodger was also a great asset when loading cattle onto a truck; if they began to balk, you just picked him up alongside the race, and he would heel them up to the front of the truck.*

However, the highlight for 1978 was Coomooroo Q-Crusader taking out the National Beef Sire of the Year award. It had been twelve years since the Angus breed took out top points, and there were 1,340 entries in the competition, which is based on the performance of progeny at major shows throughtout Australia. Q-Crusader's first progeny were exhibited in 1976 and won championships for many years afterwards. Both Coomooroo and Ben Nevis stock were taking out major awards at the shows, which was why Q-Crusader amassed an incredible 1,033 points overall. There was an amazing 43 points separating first and second place getters. It is interesting that although Dad had slowed down after he was electrocuted, the bloodlines from his breeding program were proving that he was ahead of the game and was certainly still a major contender in the industry.

It was in 1978 that Coomooroo Q-Crusader's progeny really came to the fore, when a daughter, Coomooroo Velvet, won senior and grand champion at Melbourne, and a son, Coomooroo Crusader W21, won junior and grand champion. These wins helped Coomooroo to be the most successful exhibitor at Melbourne in 1978, which followed most successful exhibitor wins at Melbourne in 1976 and Sydney in 1977.

It is a rare feat for a stud to exhibit the grand champion double, but the achievement gains even greater significance because both are by the same sire, and the awards were won in a 300-plus head display—the biggest breed section at Melbourne and the biggest Angus display in Australia in 1978.

Three other exhibitors of Q-Crusader's progeny, including Ben Nevis, also went on to win or place in the 1978 show season. At the Shepparton Show they won the all interbreed champions, both junior and senior, along with supreme beef exhibit. Dad recalls it being nine major wins, all with really good trophies, and because interbreed championships are hard to win, it was considered a huge achievement. Again, the majority of the champions were progeny of Q-Crusader.

This was a phenominal achievement for the stud and was one of the biggest highlights of Dad and Mum's stud career. Below are some memories from Sally Moore of times spent at the shows as part of Dad's team.

I travelled up in the cattle truck to the 1978 Royal Sydney Show to assist Jeff and Cliff with their show team. It was good to experience the warmer weather at a Royal Show compared to Melbourne's usual September damp. I have vivid memories of sleeping on camp stretchers on the loft above the cattle, making tea and toast with those delicious, homegrown, ripe tomatoes sliced on top for breakfast. Crossing Moore Park Road up the hill from the Sydney Show grounds to whet the whistle at the local pub was a real worry, especially when even the local policeman on duty could not be encouraged to step out to stop traffic for us; he complained a car had just run over his foot. I actually celebrated my twenty-first birthday in Sydney, so Jeff, Freddy, Wyatt, and company contrived to dunk me in the cattle trough, making sure my boots and all were completely submerged. That was okay, because it was quite hot. The trouble happened when I had to fly home that day, and although I reached Albury Terminal, my luggage went to Dubbo. When they finally found my luggage and sent it back home two weeks later, my boots were totally covered in mould!

It was also in 1978 that Dad brought to life one of his long-held visions, the Markwood Field Day, which was held on the their property. The concept of the field day was to create awareness for the Angus breed and all the diversity it offered. Dad was able to show people some of the finer qualities of the breed, demonstrate their even temperament, and showcase their conformation and versatility. It was a huge success, with people coming from far and wide to see what was on offer and why this was such a special breed of cattle.

1978: Markwood Field Day

As far as the stud was concerned, even though Dad was not as active as he had been prior to his electrocution, the stock numbers continued to increase, and it soon became evident that another move was imminent. The search began, and soon a suitable property of 179 hectares was found at Glenrowan. They made the move in December 1979. Dad's back had still not fully recovered from the electrocution (not that it ever has), but he felt his only choice at this stage was to increase the carrying capacity of the property because they were now running approximately 215 head of cattle.

Prior to leaving Markwood, Dad and Mum had a final clearing sale, and somehow Dad managed to convice the auctioneer to forego his company's commission. The value of the commission was then donated in equal amount to the Markwood Hall Committee and the Greta Football Club. The donation to the Greta Footbal Club was due to the fact that they were moving to the Greta area, and Dad thought it would be a great way to become part of the community. From this small gesture, the Greta Football Club started having an annual clearing sale of their own; Dad played an integral part in getting it established, and he was also involved with it for as long as there were residents in the area. He was one of the original committee members and worked long and hard to make the day the huge success that it was. People came from all over the district to sell their wares from the boots of their cars, or their trailers, or just by the site they were allocated. It was such a huge success that it is still running today.

CHAPTER 7

SLOWING DOWN COMES ALL TOO SOON

It was late in their first year in Glenrowan that Dad had a gallstone attack, though it was some months after the pains first started that Dad finally relented and agreed to seeing a doctor. Mum tells me that she only found out there was something wrong when he was sick enough to agree to be taken to the doctors; he had kept the pain from her all those months. He would go out onto the lawn during the night while Mum was asleep, doubled up in pain and on his hands and knees, until he could manage to go back to bed without disturbing her. Since starting my research, I have also heard that quite a few people saw him doubled over in pain during the daytime while he was out working, but he always brushed it off as nothing serious.

Dad recalls:

> *I know I had pain for months before they found out what caused it. Mum just looked at me one night, and the whites of my eyes were yellow, so she rang the doctor, and into hospital I went. They couldn't operate because of how jaundiced I was, so they sent me home again. Janet Twamley [Bob and Janet Twamley were neighbours at the time and very close friends] visited every day to give me an injection in the bum to try and get my blood right again so that they could operate at the end of the week. It was mid-November when they did the surgery. They couldn't get one of the stones because it was lodged in behind my pancreas, and I think I was in hospital for five weeks or more.*

Another neighbour, Gary Pink, was an ambulance driver who took me home so I could have Christmas with the family.

Part of the treatment for the stone they couldn't get to was to put an acid drip through a hole in my stomach to try and melt the stone or at least reduce its size. I remember the specialist and another doctor were talking, and Dr. Phillips was in the background, and I saw him just do the thumbs-down gesture as if to say this is never going to work. After about a week of the acid drip, I was allowed to go home, and when the stone shifted or whatever, the pain was so bad Cliff took me back into the hospital. I said to him, "Can this thing go any faster?" He said, "I'm doing ninety." The stone passed naturally, though, and everything was back to normal.

I remember Jeff [Junior] coming up to the hospital one night to see me. He walked in, took one look at me, and turned around and walked out again. I'd lost over three stone and wasn't looking too good.

With Dad's back the way it was, teaching cattle to lead was more challenging than it should have been. Dad, being a man full of ideas and initiative, decided he would purchase a jenny (female donkey) and let her do the hard work. He soon learnt how to make things work to his advantage and was soon tying cattle to her and letting her teach them to lead. Donkeys are stubborn and will go where they want no matter what they're dragging behind them. Word soon got around, and friends and colleagues alike were making use of Dad's latest training initiative. One year he had twenty-two head of cattle bought onto the property to be taught to lead prior to the Royal Melbourne Show. One bull that was close to two years old was brought to the property around ten days before the Melbourne Show, having never been led before, and he ended up taking out reserve senior champion, so the jenny did her job quite well!

I recall Dad having more than one clearing sale while we lived at Glenrowan. He was gradually reducing stock numbers and the accumulation of plant and equipment that he had obtained over his many years of farming. We were all very actively involved in these days, and to me they seemed to have a bit of a festive air to them. Don't get me wrong, there was always a lot of preparation in getting everything ready, and there was a lot of work to be done on the day, but something about these extra people being on the property was a fantastic thing to be a part of. Between Dad recovering from gallstones and his back injuries, Dad and Mum continued to show and breed Angus cattle, but they were definitely starting to slow down. It was while we were living at Glenrowan that I moved out of home, and by the time they made their next move, there were only two children still living at home.

One of the last shows that Dad and Mum and their team went to was the Whittlesea Feature Show in 1980, with a team of nine cattle. Dad claimed it was the hardest day of his life. Though his back pain was acute, he still managed to take out most successful exhibitor for the day! It had been a big year for the stud, with Whittlesea being the ninth show that year, including Melbourne Royal. His back pain was worse then he could endure, and it soon became evident that it was time to give up the show circuit.

They finally retired the show team in 1981, with very small teams being shown at the two Royal Shows and two rural shows. It was finally time to put away the white coats, the brushes, and the combs and to take a well-earned break. They didn't retire; they simply slowed down. The breeding program continued, and Dad contined to judge at shows and also did consulting work with other breeders. However, it soon became evident that another move was inevitable, only this time they decided they would downsize in acreage.

In January 1985 they moved to a 150-hectare property in the Kiewa Valley. The land was far more rich and fertile than the previous property at Glenrowan, and so it allowed them to run just as many cattle; it was also much closer to Wodonga. They were now selling close to one hundred bulls a year, and the proximity to Wodonga made everything much easier. Life was beginning to slow down for Dad and Mum, and with only a few children home to help run the stud, they needed to make some changes.

1986: The Kiewa Valley

53

The show team may have been retired, but within the first year on the Kiewa property they were still breeding sought-after stock; one buyer purchased thirty stud bulls in one day, which proved to be yet another industry record. By this stage they were running three hundred head of cattle, and although they were no longer showing cattle, the demand for Coomooroo stock was still as strong as ever. With the land being so productive, they were practically pasture-rearing all the stock. They sold their auger, silo, feed mill, and square baler and were making the equivalent of a couple of thousand square bales of hay a year in big, round bales.

In 1987 Coomooroo Stud sold sixteen stud heifers to the Japanese government for export to Japan. It was around this time that they met a young stock agent called Michael Glasser, who became a significant part of their lives for many years to come, not only with the buying of stock but also in the running of the Wodonga National Show and Sales.

Michael recalls:

> I remember Jeff and Pat living out at Kiewa when I first moved to the district as a stock and station agent. They weren't showing anymore, but I sometimes met up with them at the country shows and sale yards. I moved to Victorian Producers in the stud stock division in 1994, and they were then involved in the Murray Valley Angus Breeders Group, which were a proactive group of Angus breeders who used to run their own sale at Wodonga, the day after the Angus National Sale. Jeff didn't have a gruff way about him, but he did have a very persuasive way. He said, "If you can prove yourself, we'll back you," and that's how I got involved with the Murray Valley Angus Breeders Group.

Within three years of moving to Kiewa, they decided that maybe it was time to retire. They divided the property and then went on to disperse Coomooroo Angus Stud with the plan to take a long, deserved holiday and enjoy retirement. On 16 December 1988, they held the final dispersal sale on the Kiewa property, and not surprisingly it was attended by many friends, associates, and new purchasers. An estimated 300–350 people came from all over Australia for the opportunity to buy Coomooroo stock. They had 180 registered Angus cattle for sale, along with sundry plant and equipment. At the end of the day they only had seventeen heifers left and a few sundry farm items. The name and reputation of Sheather and

Coomooroo had been cemented and, along with the progeny of the Coomooroo line, would be around for many years to come due to the wide popularity of the breeding line that had been achieved over the years. And so came the end of an era. Coomooroo Angus Stud was gone but certainly never forgotten.

Over the next twelve months or so, they divided the property into seven blocks, including the house block with twenty acres—and Sheathers Lane, Wodonga, was born. While the subdivision was in progress, Dad and Mum spent a bit of time travelling around Victoria and looking at prospective places to live, and they ended up buying all the cattle from another stud that held a dispersal sale. Retirement was put on the back burner.

CHAPTER 8

RETIREMENT? NOT JUST YET

Dad recalls:

> *We purchased the complete Willara Angus Stud from down in the Western District somewhere, and with the cattle from Willara and the seventeen head of cattle we had left over from the dispersal sale, we established Trentside Angus Stud.*

It wasn't long after they purchased the cattle from the Willara Stud that Dad soon had his heart set on a property at Tarcutta.

> *We went to the auction and were the losing bidder. The owner of the property wouldn't settle on a firm price with us, and after dangling us around for four or five months, he sold the property to someone else. Anyway, on that property they had some fallow deer, and I started thinking when we get a place we'll put a few deer on it. It was not long after that we purchased the property at Hansonville. We went on to buy a few red hinds from a property at Bellbridge to take down to Hansonville.*

It was in 1989 that they purchased the Hansonville property, which consisted of 236 hectares—substantially larger than the Kiewa property, but they had both the Angus and deer now, so what choice did they have? Though they had purchased the property at Hansonville, they still had a few blocks to be sold, including the homestead, so Dad and Mum stayed in Kiewa for the first twelve months, travelling to Hansonville once a week. They initially purchased thirty-six deer, but once they decided to become involved in deer farming, off they went.

Dad was never one to do things by halves, and soon changed the stud name to Trentside Angus and Deer. He fenced two or three large paddocks to hold their growing number of deer. Although they still had Angus, as the change of name implied, the focus was now on increasing their deer numbers and on the evolving deer industry.

Dad was converting the shedding and yards on the property to be more suitable to the needs of the deer, because they were by nature quite timid animals. Dad soon found that he could handle them much easier in dark, enclosed spaces. Yards were constructed from eight-feet long pallets stood on their ends with the outsides being covered with shade cloth to reduce the light and to restrict the view the deer had, which in turn made them much easier to manage. Friends, neighbours, and family members helped in getting the property established, and it was not long after purchasing the Hansonville property that Cliff started working on the property with his wife, Fiona (known to all as Jack) and their children. After a few years Dad and Mum subdivided off five acres for Cliff and Jack to establish a home of their own.

Harvey Haigh recalls:

> I remember your Dad retiring and then buying more land when Cliff took more of an interest in farming, and then the deer farming started. They then bought a bigger property at Springhurst, and Cliff got into roses. Your Dad was left with this big property and no Cliff to help. I didn't see much of them once they left Springhurst, life being what it is.

Cliff recalls:

> I was working for Conroy's at Tallandoon when Dad purchased the Hansonville property. He believed that the property would be able to provide enough income to support two families, and so I came on board. We then lived in the house there for twelve months until Mum and Dad had sold the final blocks of the Kiewa property. Financially, however, things weren't that great, because it took much longer for the Kiewa property to sell, and interest rates were really high at the time. As a result of this, the income wasn't what it should have been, and after around

eighteen months of living on the property, I had to get a full-time job because there just wasn't enough income to support us all.

In 1991 Dad was instumental in starting the Greta Landcare Group, and he was its inaugural president; he also continued to be closely involved in the football club and its annual clearing sale. In 1992 he became a founding member and president of the Murray Deer Farmers Group, of which he was a part for many years.

Hansonville: Deer farming

Deer numbers were on the increase, and feed was on the decline due to dry conditions and the land not being suitable for growing crops They decided it was time for yet another move. Once the decision had been made to move, one of their neighbours purchased half the land, which enabled them to go ahead and purchase the next property. Mandy ended up living on the property for the two-and-half-year period it took to sell the balance of the property, which had been agisted out.

Dad recalls:

> *We use to buy truckload after truckload of feed for the deer because there wasn't enough land fenced for them to graze, so we hand-fed them a lot. We sold the cattle from Trentside Angus Stud and decided we would buy a much bigger property out at Springhurst, with the idea of fencing half the property and growing grain on the other half. Mum and I enjoyed the deer as much as anything; it was one of the better parts of our lives. They weren't overly social animals. but it was the challenge with them that made it so enjoyable. You had to have your wits about you all the time with them.*

In August 1994 they moved to a 262-hectare property just outside of Springhurst, where they ended up staying for nine years. They took all the deer fencing from the Hansonville farm with them when they moved and fenced half the new property for deer farming; the other half was cropped. It was early in their days at Springhurst that Dad became reacquanted with stock agent Michael Glasser, whom Dad and Mum had befriended while living in Kiewa.

Michael recalls;

> It wasn't that long later that Jeff and Pat started their interest in the deer industry. I began working with them even more closely. With Jeff's support I got involved with deer sales at the Wodonga Show Grounds. We had the deer sales there and were actually quite revolutionary here, I think, being the first group to use video sales with livestock. With deer being such quiet animals, we couldn't stand over them and carry out the auctions, so we had to come up with another way.

> We bought in short circuit TVs, and we had a camera in the horse stables where the deer were held. The stalls were nice and high walled, and the deer couldn't get out, but people could still walk through and view the animals. The camera man would walk along each pen, demonstrate the lot number, and film the deer while I was running the auction over in another shed, where the crowd had migrated after viewing the deer.

> We used to sell red deer, wapiti, and fallow deer at the auctions, and late one afternoon after most of the stock had been sold and picked up, we had to move a few remaining deer that weren't taken on the day to another pen overnight. Well, we were all pretty keen to go and have a beer, and Jeff said we should break this pen up a bit because the animals were a bit tight. Of course, we're in a dark shed with two big sliding doors at each end when Jeff says, "We'll just let a few out." Well, the gate got opened, and the next thing you know, all the deer are through the gate. It could have been twenty-five or thirty of them. Some of them went into the pen, and some went past it and ended up against the end sliding door! Once the deer saw a bit of light under the door, they started pushing at it, and it wasn't long before it started sliding. Jeff started yelling for someone to get the gate closed before too many got out, and the next thing I knew

there was Jeff in his blue Fairlane cutting around the racetrack and trying to head off the three escaped deer. To this day he will say he didn't know what he was going to do if he caught up with them—he was just going for it!

Anyway, the deer split up, and a couple jumped out onto Thomas Mitchell Drive and started to head into Wodonga CBD. I was young and green and had no idea what to do, so I rang the police to let them know there were a couple of red deer out on the road, to which they replied they had no time to go looking for deer because they had real problems to deal with. I then headed off out onto Thomas Mitchell Drive with Jeff now following me, and by this time the deer were at the first round-about heading down High Street. We followed them for a while and then ended up losing them over the railway line because by this time it was getting dark.

In the meantime, though, someone else had got the third deer barricaded in the horse stalls at the race track. We decided then that it was time we had the one beer that we were going to have earlier in the evening. I was still shaking like a leaf at this stage, thinking that one of these deer would cause some strife somewhere, and I'd be the one that gets into trouble. Anyway, I left the pub to go home and thought I might as well go and have another look around where we last sighted the deer, to see if I could find any sight of them. I turned a corner, and there were police cars and fire trucks everywhere. My heart just stopped! All I could think was that someone had hit one of those deer! I jumped on the CB radio and was told that something had gotten into the switch station and shorted out the power. I kept going until I got to the stop and go guy, and I asked him what's going on. He said the same thing, that something had got into the station and shorted everything out. It had blacked out half of Wodonga by this stage. I asked him what he thought had caused it, and he told me it was probably just a wombat or something like that.

In the end no one ever found out what caused the blackout, but we were quietly confident that it wasn't one of the deer, or there would have been some evidence of it. One deer was found dead on the side of the road about three weeks *later, and the other one lived very happily down at Dockers Plains for many years. That was probably the most memorable story I have about your father.*

Springhurst: Deer farming

Dad soon became a deer livestock consultant with Elders and was relied upon by them for the buying, selling, importing, and exporting deer. They soon established an auction centre at Neerim South as their central point for deer management. It was from here that they were approached by a gentleman named John who wanted to export some deer to Korea. The only problem was that he wouldn't be able to pay for them until they landed in Korea. Well, it turned out they made the deal; the deer arrived safely in Korea, but when the John arrived in Korea to collect the deer from the ship, he was promptly throw into jail. It turned out that he had done all of his paperwork in Australia, but he hadn't done any in Korea, and hence he ended up in jail and the deer were quarantined. Long story short, he got out of jail, got the deer out of quarantine, and went on to sell them in Korea. Upon returning to Australia, he ended up starting a deer compound just down the road from where Dad and Mum were living in Springhurst so that "Uncle Jeff" could help him get everything established and be his go-to guy for all things deer related in Australia. And yes, they did end up getting paid for the deer, with interest.

Michael recalls:

> *Uncle Jeff and Aunty Pat seemed to take John the Korean under their wings, even though they knew they were sticking their necks out a bit. John got his property established, and with no small amount of help from Uncle Jeff, he soon had a well-established deer compound set up for buying and exporting deer to Korea. Anyway, it was within a few short years that things went sour for John, and his bank ended up foreclosing on*

his loans. It got to the stage that the sheriff was asked to go out and take control of the stock and property, which was to be sold off to clear debts.

The sheriff rings your Dad because of his involvement and knowledge of the property, and he asks him bring some men and meet them out at the property early one morning. We arrived before sunrise this morning to meet the sheriff and get our instructions. The sheriff said we were all going to drive onto the property. He would serve the papers, and then we were all to head down to the yards to do a count of the animals and plant. So the papers get served, and we head down the yards, get the deer in, and start counting them when John turns up with a stay of execution. So we pack up and head off the property, where the sheriff promptly produces some mugs, a thermos of tea, and some scones for us. He then went on to compliment us on how well we handled ourselves and offered us the opportunity to work with him again the following Saturday morning as his strongmen! Needless to say, there was a quick no from Uncle Jeff.

Dad and Mum spent alot of their time helping out not only John but many other people when it came to buying and selling deer. They were in deer farming for about twelve years, and as Dad was approaching seventy years of age, they realised it was about time they seriously thought about retiring. Dad believes that they were lucky in that they got into deer farming at the right time—and even more important, they got out at the right time, too. The property was put on the market in August 2002 when they were running between eight hundred and a thousand head of deer, which were available for sale with the property. The property itself was sold quite quickly, with the deer being sold between the property sale and settlement date. They then moved to their next property on 15 January 2003.

CHAPTER 9

FINALLY THEY DO RETIRE, BUT NOT AS PLANNED

Dad and Mum moved to a beautiful property consisting of 40 hectares of land with 139 hectares of government lease riverflats at Killawarra. They planned to still run a few cattle, but for them this was the start of retirement. Dad celebrated his seventieth birthday eleven days later, and life started to slow down for them. They soon realised they needed some type of hobby and so began to breed birds. Over the next few years, what started out as one aviary of parrots became a network of avaries with many different types of birds. Between managing the farm and looking after all the birds they had purchased and bred, they found that this occupied enough of their time, and they were very comfortable with their lifestyle.

It was during this time at Killawarra that Dad decided he would create his own super-breed of cattle. He was going to cross-breed between four different breeds of cattle to eventually get an animal that was the best of all breeds.

Dad recalls:

> I was using Charolais, Angus, and Limousin, and my secret weapon was going to be Guernsey. I had four Guernsey cows and four Charolais cows, Limousin, and Angus bulls, and I was going to cross-breed them. While using dairy cows for foster mothers, I found that Guernseys were the best producers of the right type of milk to grow stud cattle, and I was going to use a quarter Guernsey, a quarter Limousin, a quarter Charolais, and a quarter Angus, mixing the four breeds together. The

65

Guersey was my secret weapon. People will try cross-breeding, but no one would think about using Guernseys. I purchased my Guerney and Charolais cows and a Limousin bull and started the breeding program but I never got to see any results because the calves weren't on the ground when I got crook.

Life was very happy for Dad and Mum until early in 2006, when Dad had a fall down on the river flats while moving some cattle. Though the details are not quite clear, it is believed that Dad somehow had a fall, hit his head on a log, and lost consciousness for a short period. When Mum got to him, he was conscious but a bit foggy. Mum helped him to the car and drove him back up to the house. (This in itself was amazing to us, because to this day I have never seen my mother drive.) From here he seemed to develop flu-like symptoms that got worse over the following months. The doctors had no idea what was going on but agreed that it was very flu-like, even though he was gradually getting worse.

Dad—2003 on the left and in 2007 on the right

Within three months of having the fall, he was hospitalised because his health had deteriorated so much. He was using a walking cane to get around, and tests showed that his brain function had slowed down so much that his response time was like that of a ninety-year-old. The first time I saw him in hospital, I was shocked. He had lost quite a bit of weight, was withdrawn, was not eating, and was so soft-spoken that it was an effort to hear him. Anyone that has ever known Dad would liken him to a big, loud bull, but now he was like a small, newborn calf. It was really distressing to see—he had virtually withdrawn into himself.

Rosie recalls:

> *When I went up to the hospital, he was really vague and couldn't remember basic, everyday things; it was almost like he had suffered a stroke. When he came home from the hospital, I went out to the farm every Sunday and drove him around the property so that he could check on things, and I'd do whatever needed to be done. I remember him being really weak, but he seemed to grow stronger when he had things to occupy his mind, like organising the clearing sale and the sale of the property.*

I remember the way the nurses treated him being really poor; to them, it seemed he was just an old man on his last leg who needed basic care. The thing of it was that the more he was treated like an old man, the more he seemed to behave like one. The saddest thing was that he had a few bedsores and really bad mouth ulcers that were preventing him from chewing his food, so he had stopped eating. The nurses didn't know any of this because they hadn't made the effort to find out what was going on. Mum and I brought him in a lambswool from home to lie on and got the staff to organise some treatment for his mouth; we arranged for his food to be blended until he could eat properly again, which made a big difference to his ability to start getting better.

We also took in a family photo, which included both Dad and Mum, their children with partners, and grandchildren to put on Dad's overbed table, to remind him of how many people loved him. It was amazing, the way the attitude of the nursing staff changed after being told that all those people in the photos were this sick man's children and grandchildren, and that he had been a very loud and active man just a few months earlier. I believe his health care improved quite significantly from that day onwards, and after seeing many specialists Dad was eventually diagnosed with lupus.

Lupus (also referred to as SLE, or systemic lupus erythematosus) is an autoimmune disease, that takes on several forms and can affect any part of the body, but it most commonly attacks the skin, joints, heart, lungs, blood, kidneys, and brain. There is no cure for lupus, though symptoms can be treated with drugs such as corticosteroids and immunosuppressants. Apparently nearly 90 per cent of lupus patients are women aged between fifteen to forty-five, so it certainly was not something the doctors were looking for. I've been told if you have five of the eleven common symptoms for lupus, there is a fair chance you have the disease. Dad had all eleven symptoms. I remember when he finally came home from the hospital and was more educated in the disease and what was happening to his body, he said that each day he felt like a different part of his body was being attacked.

As a result of Dad's illness, the stock was sold, including the cows that were carrying the new super-breed calves. The birds and avaries were given to Cliff and his son Blake, and the property was put on the market. So much had happened in such a short time: in twelve months their lives had been turned completely upside down. Dad had gone from being an active and healthy farmer to a shadow of his former self. I am thrilled to say his brain function has improved enormously and continues to improve every day, but back in 2007 there really was no choice but to accept that the farming life was over, and they decided to move into Wangaratta.

CHAPTER 10

TOWN LIFE

This was the first residential property that Mum and Dad had owned their entire married life. Fortunately, they settled into town life quite quickly and seemed to have visitors all the time.

Mandy recalls:

> *Dad had always been busy, always planning or doing things, and when they moved into Wangaratta he continued to plan, but he now got others to do the things he couldn't do. He got Cliff to build them vegetable gardens that one didn't have to bend down to work in, and they had Rosie establish and plant gardens. They were making improvements as they had with all properties, but on a smaller scale.*

Rosie was also integral in their care at this stage, because she was living nearby just out of Benalla. She was with Dad and Mum at least once a week. She helped around the house, took them to doctors' appointment, and took Mum grocery shopping. She was there for them in every way they needed.

Rosie recalls:

> *They moved to Wangaratta, and Dad seemed to be really flat again because there weren't enough things to be done around the place. He used to have a list for me every time I turned up, and now he no longer made lists. When they then made the decision to move to Wodonga, he*

seemed to brighten up again, as there were more things to do. His lists started again.

I was working five days a week and doing evening meetings at the time, but I had a day at home and a day with Mum and Dad to do things with them and for them. I then moved to Queensland, and Rita and Mandy picked up where I'd left off.

When Rosie moved to Queensland late in 2008, Rita and Mandy started travelling down from Wodonga to help with appointments and groceries. This went on for about a year until Dad and Mum decided that maybe moving to Wangaratta hadn't really been the right place to relocate to. In August 2010 they put their property on the market and started looking for a house in Wodonga.

Finally they were moving back home to Wodonga, where they'd first met, where they were married, where they both had siblings, and where they were close to Rita and Mandy. It was the best move they could have made, and I believe they seem happier now than they have in a long time. Wodonga really is where they belong, surrounded by people they love and that love them. It is only a few hours' drive away for me and Brenda; Cliff is about an hour away, and now Paul also lives in Wodonga. That's six children that live close enough to see them regularly. Their other five children all live in Queensland, but never does a week go by without a phone call to see how things are going.

Over the months in 2012 and 2013 we have had quite a few day trips, visiting places from Dad and Mum's past. It has been a wonderful trip down memory lane, and it has helped enormously with the writing of this book.

As sad as it is that Dad got sick and gave up so much, if it had not happened, then I would not have had the inspiration to write this book over the past seven years. As a matter of fact, it was soon after coming home from the hospital that Dad asked me to record some of his memories. I told him I would do one better than that: I would write a book around his memories. This experience has given me an insight into my parents that I believe few children have the opportunity to glimpse, and I have learned so much from these two people whom I have always loved so dearly.

Through all the time we have shared putting together this book, Dad and Mum have taught me about strength, courage, and endurance. What wonderful lessons to have learned through such an remarkable journey. They are both amazing people who have achieved more than I would have dreamed possible.

Thank you both for all that you are and all that you have given.

2013—Dad's 80th birthday

ABOUT THE AUTHOR

I am the seventh of eleven children, and in my family, growing up wasn't the survival of the fittest—it was the survival of the loudest. By being loud one is heard—well, eventually!

As an adult I live in a small country town in Victoria with my husband and our two dogs. We have two grown-up children who both live nearby. I enjoy reading, photography, and gardening when I have the time.